EYEWITNESS TO
THE TREATY OF
VERSAILLES

BY NICK REBMAN

Published by The Child's World®
1980 Lookout Drive • Mankato, MN 56003-1705
800-599-READ • www.childsworld.com

Photographs ©: AP Images, cover, 1, 9, 16; National Archives/Handout/MCT/
Newscom, 5; Picture History/Newscom, 6; Harris & Ewing/Library of Congress, 10,
20; Mirrorpix/Newscom, 11; World History Archive/Newscom, 12, 14, 19; akg-images/
Newscom, 22, 25; Everett Historical/Shutterstock Images, 26, 28

ISBN 9781503816084

LCCN 2016945633

Printed in the United States of America
PA02317

ABOUT THE AUTHOR

Nick Rebman enjoys reading, drawing, and traveling to places where he
doesn't speak the language. He lives in Minnesota.

TABLE OF
CONTENTS

FAST FACTS

What was the Treaty of Versailles?

- The **Treaty** of Versailles was a peace treaty between the victorious Allies and the defeated Germans at the end of World War I (1914–1918).

Who wrote the Treaty of Versailles?

- Leaders of the Allied countries wrote the treaty.
- Three leaders made most of the decisions. They were Woodrow Wilson of the United States, Georges Clemenceau of France, and David Lloyd George of the United Kingdom.

Where was the Treaty of Versailles written?

- The Allies' leaders met in Paris, France, to write the treaty.
- The treaty was signed in Versailles, France, a city near Paris.

When was the Treaty of Versailles created?

- The peace conference began in January 1919 and lasted for several months.
- The Treaty of Versailles was signed on June 28, 1919.

Why was the Treaty of Versailles necessary?

- Fighting in World War I ended in November 1918, but there was a chance it could start up again if an agreement between the two sides was not reached.

- The Treaty of Versailles officially ended World War I.

Chapter 1

PEACE AT LAST

In December 1918, Woodrow Wilson stepped off his steamship and onto French soil. World War I was finally over. Now, with the Central powers defeated, it was time for a peace conference. Wilson was the president of the United States. He had traveled across the Atlantic Ocean to take part in the conference. All the leaders of the victorious Allied nations were there with him. They met in Paris, the French capital.

Wilson took off his top hat and greeted the other Allied leaders. They planned to create a separate treaty for each of the defeated nations. These nations included Germany, Austria-Hungary, and the Ottoman Empire. But the Central powers were not invited to the meetings. That meant they would have no input on the Allies' decisions. They would have to accept whatever terms the Allies laid out.

Wilson had high hopes for the conference. His plan for peace was known as the Fourteen Points. He had been talking about it for months. The Fourteen Points applied to many countries, including Germany. The plan would result in "a just and stable peace," Wilson said.[1] He believed this approach would prevent future wars. He also believed Germany should not face harsh punishment. German leaders knew about Wilson's plan. They thought it seemed fair.

Wilson entered his office in the house where he was staying. Two other men soon joined him. One was Georges Clemenceau, the leader of France. The other was David Lloyd George, the leader of the United Kingdom. These men became known as the Big Three. More than 20 nations were taking part in the Paris meetings. But the Big Three dominated the peace conference.

They made all the major decisions by themselves.

Wilson sat in his armchair and started to speak. The treaty with Germany should follow the Fourteen Points, he said. Clemenceau sat back in his chair, adjusting his gloves. He strongly disagreed with Wilson. During the war, France had suffered greatly at the hands of Germany. As a result, Clemenceau wanted to punish Germany harshly. In particular, he wanted to make sure Germany stayed weak. That way Germany would be unable to attack France again. Clemenceau also wanted to force Germany to make huge payments for the damage it had caused.

Lloyd George stood up and tried to smooth over the disagreement. He understood both men's concerns. The United Kingdom had also suffered greatly because of Germany. Before the conference, Lloyd George had agreed with Clemenceau.

> "It must be a peace without victory. . . . Victory would mean peace forced upon the loser. . . . It would be accepted in humiliation. . . . Only a peace between equals can last."
>
> —*Woodrow Wilson*[2]

Artillery and aircraft heavily damaged many cities in France, ▶ including Paris.

Lloyd George had said Germany deserved to be treated harshly. But now, in Paris, the British leader softened his tone. He still wanted payments, but he did not want to punish Germany too much. He wanted Germany's economy to be strong. That would be good for people throughout Europe, he said.

▲ **David Lloyd George feared a harsh punishment for Germany would lead to another war.**

▲ **The Big Three (from left to right), David Lloyd George, Georges Clemenceau, and Woodrow Wilson, at the peace conference in France in June 1919.**

The talks went on for hours. By evening, the men had made little progress. They agreed to meet again the next day. The Allied leaders had different goals, and they spent months negotiating. In May 1919, they finally reached an agreement. None of the Big Three had gotten everything he wanted. But a draft of the peace treaty with Germany was ready at last. Now there was only one question remaining. Would Germany sign it?

Chapter 2

WAR GUILT

It was a lovely spring day in Versailles, France. The flowers were in bloom, and bird songs filled the air. It was May 7, 1919. Germany's leaders arrived at a beautiful hotel. They walked inside and took their seats in the hotel's meeting room. For the first time, they would hear the terms of the treaty the Allies had written.

◄ **The initial talks between German and Allied officials took place at Trianon Palace in Versailles.**

Clemenceau stood up and began the meeting. "You have asked for peace," he said to the German leaders. "We are ready to give you peace."[3] Clemenceau then explained everything the Big Three had decided. He explained that Germany had to limit its army to 100,000 soldiers. The German leaders looked at one another with concern. This would be a major change. During the war, millions of soldiers had been in the German army.

Clemenceau continued. Germany was not allowed to build war equipment such as tanks and submarines, he said. Also, large parts of western Germany had to be completely free of soldiers and military equipment.

The German leaders shifted in their seats. They were not happy, but they were not surprised. They knew smaller armies were a top priority. People throughout Europe believed large militaries had been one of the causes of the war. Even the Allies had agreed to reduce their militaries over time.

But Clemenceau was not done speaking. He said Germany had to admit it was responsible "for causing all the loss and damage" of the war.[4] That meant Germany also had to pay billions of dollars in **reparations**.

▲ **Delegates meet in the Trianon Palace to discuss the conditions of the Treaty of Versailles.**

Economists had warned the Big Three about reparations. Forcing Germany to make huge payments would be a disaster, they had said. Germany would never be able to make the payments, and it would disrupt the world economy. But Clemenceau did not want Germany to have the strength to attack France again.

Clemenceau finished his speech and waited. The head of the German delegation, Ulrich von Brockdorff-Rantzau, sat at the table, his knees shaking. As a show of disrespect, he refused to stand when speaking. "We are required to admit that we alone are war-guilty," he said from his chair. "Such an admission on my lips would be a lie."[5]

The Germans had expected the treaty to be based on the Fourteen Points. But the Allies had given them a treaty that had little in common with Wilson's plan. The Germans believed the "war guilt" section was completely unfair. They believed the Allies were ignoring the true cause of the war. The conflict had started as a dispute between Austria-Hungary and Serbia. Germany was pulled into the conflict because it was Austria-Hungary's ally.

> "If I were a German, I think I should never sign it."
>
> —*Woodrow Wilson, speaking about the Treaty of Versailles*[6]

Even so, the Allies insisted on their terms. They gave Germany two weeks to decide whether to sign the treaty.

Chapter 3

LEAGUE OF NATIONS

Wilson could not believe his eyes. As he peered out the window of his car, he saw destruction all around him. Wilson was touring Belgium. He had a few days off while Germany considered the treaty. Wilson looked at the piles of rubble. The war had devastated Belgium. He found it hard to imagine that this area had once been a city.

◀ **Ypres, Belgium, was the site of numerous major battles during World War I. The city was reduced to rubble by artillery fire.**

The war's destruction had not been limited to Europe. Fighting had also taken place in Africa and Asia. In all, millions of people had been killed. Wilson wanted to make sure this kind of tragedy never happened again.

In Paris, Wilson had compromised on many parts of the treaty. But there was one thing he had not been willing to give up. Now as he looked at the ruins, he was glad he had worked so hard to make the League of Nations part of the treaty.

The League of Nations would be an organization dedicated to world peace. The idea was that all countries would guarantee one another's safety. That would discourage countries from starting conflicts. Any country that went to war would be punished economically. Physical force would be used only when necessary. "That is the last resort," Wilson said, "because this is intended as a constitution of peace, not as a league of war."[7]

When Wilson returned to Paris, he learned that Germany was refusing to sign the treaty. German leaders demanded that certain parts be changed. The Allies sent a response. There would be no changes to the treaty. And if Germany refused to sign it, the Allies would resume the war.

17

Germany's deadline was hours away. But still the Allies heard no reply. Finally, with only two hours to go, Germany agreed to sign the treaty.

The day had finally arrived. On June 28, 1919, Wilson entered the Palace of Versailles. He made his way to the building's famous Hall of Mirrors. Sunlight flooded into the crowded room. The hall was filled with politicians and reporters. After greeting Clemenceau, Wilson watched as the Germans entered the room.

Two German leaders approached the table and sat down. "It was as if men were called upon to sign their own death warrants," said a member of Wilson's staff.[8] The men's faces were pale. Their hands shook nervously as they signed the treaty. The document became known as the Treaty of Versailles because of the city in which it was signed.

The German leaders quickly left the building. But for the Allies, it was a day of celebration. World War I was officially over!

The next day, Wilson boarded his steamship and set off for the United States. The voyage took more than a week. That gave him plenty of time to think. He knew the U.S. Constitution required the Senate to **ratify** all treaties before they took effect.

Despite intense protests in Germany, German officials signed ▶ the Treaty of Versailles on June 28, 1919.

▲ Republican senators (from left to right)
William Borah, Henry Cabot Lodge,
and Reed Smoot strongly opposed the
League of Nations.

That meant the United States would not become a member of the League of Nations unless the Senate ratified the Treaty of Versailles.

Wilson arrived in the United States on July 8. Thousands of people lined the streets to cheer him on. Wilson was glad to be home. But there was no time to relax. He had a speech to prepare for.

Two days later, Wilson spoke to the Senate. If the United States rejected the treaty, it would "break the heart of the world," he said.[9] But many senators were not convinced. They thought the League of Nations would force the United States to take part in foreign wars. That was a risk the leaders were unwilling to take.

> "I am, as everyone knows, not only in favor of a League of Nations, but believe the formation of such a League absolutely indispensable to the maintenance of peace."
>
> —*Woodrow Wilson*[10]

Debate went on for months. Finally, in November, the Senate was ready to decide. The vote was not even close. The Senate rejected the treaty.

It was a bitter defeat for Wilson. His dream of a League of Nations was finally a reality. But the United States was not a member.

Chapter 4

CHANGES IN TERRITORY

A farmer headed out to his field for another day of work. As he tended to his crops, he thought about all the changes that had taken place recently. Last year, in 1918, he had been a German man living in Germany. Now, in 1919, he was a Polish man living in Poland. The farmer had not moved. But Germany's borders had.

Life was not easy for the farmer. He still thought of himself as German. But most people in the area considered themselves Polish. The farmer was a minority. As a result, his neighbors often treated him cruelly. Just last week, someone had set his barn on fire.

In the evening, the weary farmer returned to his house. He sat in his favorite chair and opened the newspaper. His eye was drawn to a new map of Europe. It looked so different from the map he was used to seeing. The Treaty of Versailles had greatly reshaped Europe's borders. The country of Poland had not existed before the war. But now Poland took up a large chunk of Germany's old territory in the east. In the west, France had also gained parts of Germany.

> "Unsettling events began to swirl around my parents' farm. More and more of my mother's chickens had begun disappearing as had the livestock of other neighboring German families."
>
> —Christel Weiss Brandenburg, whose family farm went from being in Germany to Poland after the Treaty of Versailles[11]

23

Denmark and Belgium had taken small bits of German territory as well. In all, Germany lost approximately 27,000 square miles (70,000 sq km) of land and 7 million people.

The farmer noticed that governments were changing, too. Before the war, Germany had been a **monarchy**. Now it was a **democracy**. The farmer turned the page of his newspaper. He realized Europe was not the only place with new borders and new governments. Similar changes were happening all over the world. Before the war, Germany had controlled **colonies** in Africa and Asia. But the Treaty of Versailles took those colonies away from Germany. Now the League of Nations was putting Allied countries in charge.

The Allied countries created new governments in Germany's former colonies. They made many promises. The people who lived there would receive better education and health care. The new governments would also focus on better transportation and utilities. The eventual goal, the Allied leaders said, was to prepare these former colonies for **independence**.

The farmer folded his newspaper and went to bed. In the years that followed, the farmer continued to keep an eye on the news. By the 1960s, the farmer was an old man.

Governments were changing again. Many of Germany's former colonies were finally gaining their independence. It had been more than 40 years after the Treaty of Versailles was signed.

▲ **After World War I ended, many soldiers in German colonies were released with no pay for their service.**

Chapter 5

VIOLATING THE TREATY

A woman and her husband discussed the Treaty of Versailles as they ate a simple dinner. Like most people in Germany, they hated the treaty. The year was 1923. Germany could not afford its payments to the Allies, just as the economists had predicted. As a result, the country's economy was crumbling. Everyday goods were extremely expensive. Many people could barely afford to buy food.

◄ **Because of the poor economy, German money had little value. Some Germans resorted to trading objects.**

After dinner the couple went to a political rally. A politician named Adolf Hitler took the stage. He was the leader of a small group called the Nazi Party. Hitler's speech electrified the crowd. He blamed the Treaty of Versailles for Germany's troubles. "The treaty was made in order to bring 20 million Germans to their deaths and to ruin the German nation," Hitler said.[12]

Many Germans liked what they heard. They wanted a strong leader who would reject the Treaty of Versailles. More important, they wanted someone who would restore Germany's dignity.

> "This is not peace. It is an **armistice** for 20 years."
>
> —French general Ferdinand Foch, speaking about the Treaty of Versailles in 1919[13]

Hitler gained many strong supporters among the people of Germany. The Nazi Party grew into the most powerful party in Germany. In the 1930s, Hitler took control of Germany's government.

Hitler wanted to make the country stronger, so he built up Germany's military. He also sent troops into western Germany. Both of these actions were strictly forbidden by the Treaty of Versailles.

Despite Hitler's actions, the League of Nations did nothing to stop them. The world was on the brink of a second world war.

THINK ABOUT IT

- During World War I, Germany caused major destruction in France. Do you think Georges Clemenceau was right to demand that Germany be treated harshly?
- The Treaty of Versailles forced Germany to give up its colonies in Africa and Asia. How do you think this affected the people who lived in these colonies?
- Why do you think the League of Nations did nothing to stop Hitler in the 1930s? What concerns do you think the League of Nations had?

◀ **Adolf Hitler (center) promised to overturn the Treaty of Versailles.**

GLOSSARY

armistice (AHR-mi-stis): An armistice is a truce in which two sides agree to stop fighting for a time. The Allies and the Central powers signed an armistice in November 1918.

colonies (KAH-luh-neez): Colonies are areas controlled by a more powerful country. In the early 1900s, Germany had colonies in Africa and Asia.

democracy (di-MAH-kruh-see): Democracy is a system of government in which people choose their leaders by voting. Germany became a democracy after World War I ended.

economy (i-KAHN-uh-mee): An economy is a system of buying and selling goods. Germany's economy suffered greatly after the Treaty of Versailles.

independence (in-de-PEN-dens): Independence is when a country controls its own government. Poland received its independence after World War I.

monarchy (MAH-nar-kee): Monarchy is a system of government in which a king or queen has power. Germany was a monarchy during World War I.

ratify (RAT-uh-fy): Ratify means to give approval to a treaty and make it law. The U.S. Senate refused to ratify the Treaty of Versailles.

reparations (reh-puh-RAY-shunz): Reparations are payments for damage caused during a war. The Treaty of Versailles forced Germany to pay reparations.

treaty (TREE-tee): A treaty is an official agreement between two or more countries. A peace treaty is a document that puts an official end to a war.

SOURCE NOTES

1. "President Woodrow Wilson's Fourteen Points." *The Avalon Project*. Lillian Goldman Law Library, 2008. Web. 22 Jun. 2016.

2. "We Need a Peace Without Victory." *Guardian*. Guardian News and Media, 13 Nov. 2008. Web. 22 Jun. 2016.

3. "Antagonists Face to Face." *Guardian*. Guardian News and Media, 13 Nov. 2008. Web. 22 Jun. 2016.

4. Ibid.

5. John Milton Cooper. *Woodrow Wilson*. New York: Knopf, 2009. Print. 495.

6. Ann Hagedorn. *Savage Peace: Hope and Fear in America, 1919*. New York: Simon & Schuster, 2007. Print. 264.

7. John Milton Cooper. *Woodrow Wilson*. New York: Knopf, 2009. Print. 475.

8. Ibid. 503–504.

9. John Milton Cooper. *Breaking the Heart of the World*. Cambridge, UK: Cambridge UP, 2001. Print. 9.

10. John Milton Cooper. *Woodrow Wilson*. New York: Knopf, 2009. Print. 464.

11. Christel Weiss Brandenburg. *Ruined by the Reich*. Jefferson, NC: McFarland & Co., 2003. Print. 19–20.

12. "Nazi Conspiracy and Aggression Volume 1, Chapter VII." *The Avalon Project*. Lillian Goldman Law Library, 2008. Web. 22 Jun. 2016.

13. Kennedy Hickman. "World War I: Marshal Ferdinand Foch" *About Education*. About, 2016. Web. 2 Aug. 2016.

TO LEARN MORE

Books

Grant, R. G. *World War I: The Definitive Visual History: From Sarajevo to Versailles*. New York: DK, 2014.

Swayze, Alan. *The End of World War I: The Treaty of Versailles and Its Tragic Legacy*. New York: Crabtree, 2014.

Venezia, Mike. *Woodrow Wilson*. New York: Children's Press, 2007.

Web Sites

Visit our Web site for links about the Treaty of Versailles:
childsworld.com/links

Note to Parents, Teachers, and Librarians: We routinely verify our Web links to make sure they are safe and active sites. So encourage your readers to check them out!

INDEX